AUTORI

Paolo Crippa (23 April 1978) has been cultivating a passion for Italian history since the time of high school, especially during the Second World War. His research focuses mainly on the field of military history and in particular on armored units from the 1930s until the end of the Second World War. In 2006 he published his first volume, "I Reparti Corazzati della Repubblica Sociale Italiana 1943/1945", the first organic research carried out and published in Italy on the subject, followed by " Duecento Volti della R.S.I." (2007) and "Un anno con il 27° Reggimento Artiglieria Legnano" (2011). He has about forty articles for the magazines Milites, Historica Nuova, SGM - Second World War, Batailes & Blindes, Mezzi Corazzati, Storia & Battaglie and Storia del XX Secolo, both as an author and in collaboration with other researchers and he has created collaborations and consultancy for other authors in the drafting of historical - uniformological texts. From 2019 he collaborates with Luca Cristini Editore in the realization of the "Witness to War" series and from 2020 he is the Director. With Mattioli 1885 he published "Italy 43-45. Civil War's improvised AFVsr" (2014), " Italian AFVs of the Civil War 1943 - 1945" (2015) and "Italy 43-45. AFVs and MVs of the cobelligerent units "(2018).

Luigi Manes (18th July 1966) has already published four books: "British tracked carriers of World War Two" (Soldiershop Publishing, 2019), "The Sherman medium tank in the European theater of operations" (Soldiershop Publishing, 2019), "Italy 43-45 – AFV's and MV's of co-belligerent units"(Mattioli 1885, 2018) with Paolo Crippa and "Carri armati Sherman in Sicilia" (Edizioni Ardite, 2018) with Lorenzo Bovi. He has written various articles, both for the military modeling magazine "Steel Art" and the website "ModellismoPiù". Always interested in the history of Second World War, he has a great passion for the Sherman medium tank from an historical and technological point of view.

PUBLISHING'S NOTES

None of unpublished images or text of our book may be reproduced in any format without the expressed written permission of Luca Cristini Editore (already Soldiershop.com) when not indicate as marked with license creative commons 3.0 or 4.0. Luca Cristini Editore has made every reasonable effort to locate, contact and acknowledge rights holders and to correctly apply terms and conditions to Content.
Every effort has been made to trace the copyright of all the photographs. If there are unintentional omissions, please contact the publisher in writing at: info@soldiershop.com, who will correct all subsequent editions.
Our trademark: Luca Cristini Editore@, and the names of our series & brand: Soldiershop, Witness to war, Museum book, Bookmoon, Soldiers&Weapons, Battlefield, War in colour, Historical Biographies, Darwin's view, Fabula, Altrastoria, Italia Storica Ebook, Witness To History, Soldiers, Weapons & Uniforms, Storia etc. are herein @ by Luca Cristini Editore.

LICENSES COMMONS

This book may utilize part of material marked with license creative commons 3.0 or 4.0 (CC BY 4.0), (CC BY-ND 4.0), (CC BY-SA 4.0) or (CC0 1.0). We give appropriate attribution credit and indicate if change were made in the acknowledgments field. Our WTW books series utilize only fonts licensed under the SIL Open Font License or other free use license.

For a complete list of Soldiershop titles please contact Luca Cristini Editore on our website: www.soldiershop.com or www.cristinieditore.com. E-mail: info@soldiershop.com

Title: **YUGOSLAVIAN ARMORED UNITS 1940-1945** Code.: **WTW-012 EN** By Paolo Crippa & Luigi Manes
ISBN code: 978-88-93275958 First edition May 2020. Brand director: Paolo Crippa
Text: English Nr. of images: 133 Layout: 177,8x254mm Cover & Art Design: Luca S. Cristini
WITNESS TO WAR (SOLDIERSHOP) is a trademark of Luca Cristini Editore, via Orio, 35/4 - 24050 Zanica (BG) ITALY.

WITNESS TO WAR

YUGOSLAVIAN ARMORED UNITS 1940 -1945

KINGDOM OF YUGOSLAVIA - INDEPENDENT STATE OF CROATIA - CROATIAN WEHRMACHT UNITS - SLOVENIAN DOMOBRANCI

PHOTOS & IMAGES FROM WORLD WARTIME ARCHIVES

PAOLO CRIPPA - LUIGI MANES

BOOKS TO COLLECT

CONTENTS

Armored fighting vehicles of the Yugoslavian Royal Army..................5
   Creation and development of armored units..................5
   The Second World War..................5
   Colors of Yugoslavian armored fighting vehicles..................9
Croatian armored units..................35
   Croatian units..................38
      Tank Company of the 1st Ustaša Brigade..................38
      Tank Company of the 3rd Ustaša Brigade..................38
      Tank Company of the 4th Ustaša Brigade..................38
      Tank Company of the 5th Ustaša Brigade..................38
      Tank Companies of the P.T.B. 39
      Ustaša Obrana (Ustaša Defense Unit)..................40
      1st Light Tank Company of the 1st Mountain Division..................40
      Tank Platoon of the 1st Mountain Brigade..................40
      Tank Platoon of the 3rd Mountain Brigade..................40
      Tank Platoon of the 4th Mountain Brigade..................40
      Tank Platoon of the 3rd Jäger Brigade..................40
      Tank Platoon of the 4th Jäger Brigade..................41
      Light Tank Company..................41
      Armored Reserve Company
      (also referred to as Armored Reserve Command)..................41
      3rd Corps Tank Platoon..................41
      Light Tank Platoon of the 1st Transport Battalion..................41
   "Oklopni Samovoz" improvised armored fighting vehicles..................41
   Colors of Croatian armored fighting vehicles..................42
Croatian armored units dependent on the German Armed Forces..................81
   369. (Kroatische) Infanterie-Division (369. (Hrvatska) Pješacka Divizija)..................81
   373. (Kroatische) Infanterie-Division (373. (Hrvatska) Pješacka Divizija)..................81
   392. (Kroatische) Infanterie-Division (392. (Hrvatska) Pješacka Divizija)..................82
Slovenian armored fighting vehicles..................89
   Colors of Slovenian armored fighting vehicles..................89
Bibliography..................97

ARMORED FIGHTING VEHICLES OF THE YUGOSLAVIAN ROYAL ARMY

Creation and development of armored units

The creation of the first armored units for the Army of the Kingdom of Yugoslavia dates back to the late 1920s, when, on the basis of the experiences gained by the armies engaged in trench warfare during the Great War, military authorities felt the need to provide formations with an armored component. Contrary to what happened with many other European armies at that time, these armored formations did not develop as an extension of the cavalry divisions but were instead formed as independent units, officially called "Combat Units". Tanks were consequently identified with the term "combat vehicles"[1]. The first armored vehicles used by Yugoslavia were 11 Renault FT-17 and 10 Renault-Kegresse M-28 tanks[2] (11 according to other sources), received from France in 1929.

In the first half of the 1930s, the Yugoslavian Royal Army began a process of reforming its two Cavalry Divisions, with the aim of increasing their offensive potential. These two divisions consisted of 2 or 3 Cavalry Brigades on 2 Regiments each, a horse-drawn Artillery Squadron, a Cyclist Battalion and other support units. It was therefore planned to include a Motorized Regiment in both divisions, reinforced with vehicles such as light tanks or tankettes. The problem of finding the necessary armored vehicles arose from the beginning, since the local industry was unable to produce tanks. Thanks to the good degree of military cooperation between France and Yugoslavia, the Yugoslavians were able to place orders with the French for armored vehicles. France, however, was unwilling to sell its more modern tanks and, at the same time, had the need to get rid of oldest models. To expand its armored vehicle fleet, Yugoslavia imported, probably from Poland, another 14 Renault FT-17s in 1932. Finally, about 20 FT-17s (in bad condition) were obtained from France, in the form of military aid, between 1935 and 1936. The Combat Vehicle Battalion was established with these tanks in 1936. This unit, often mistakenly referred to as the 1st Battalion, was divided into 3 Companies, each formed of 3 Platoons. Each platoon had 3 tanks and another 21 tanks formed the Battalion Reserve, for a total of 48 between FT-17s and M-28s.

The Second World War

With the outbreak of the Second World War, it became almost impossible for the Yugoslavian Royal Army to acquire new tanks to supplement its scarce armored force. The military authorities, however, were not discouraged and continued negotiations with France, which, at the beginning of 1940, agreed to sell 54 R-35 light tanks to Yugoslavia. The R-35s were indeed relatively more modern vehicles than the old FT-17s. Delivered in April, these tanks were the

---

[1] Interestingly, the Yugoslavian Royal Army never adopted the term "tank" and instead referred to these vehicles simply as "combat vehicles" ("Борбено возило").
[2] Also known as Renault NC Kegresse, an unfortunate development of the old FT-17, with which it shared great part of the mechanical system.

last armored vehicles that arrived in Yugoslavia before the German invasion of France blocked any hope of future purchases. Therefore, on the eve of the conflict, the Yugoslavian Army could count on a really small armored component, including just over a hundred armored vehicles[3]:

- Renault FT-17 tanks = about 45
- Renault-Kegresse M-28 tanks = 10/11
- Renault R-35 tanks = 54
- T-32 (Š-I-D) self-propelled guns = 8
- Automitrailleuse White M1918 armored cars = 2
- SPA armored cars[4] = 2

On May 3, 1940, the Combat Vehicle Battalion was split into two units, named 1st and 2nd Combat Vehicle Battalion respectively. The 1st Battalion was equipped with older FT-17s and M-28s, while the newly purchased R-35 tanks were assigned to the 2nd Battalion[5]. Each Battalion was divided into 3 Companies of 3 Platoons and, besides the tanks, both units had motorized vehicles for the transporting ammunition and spare parts. Infantry, artillery or anti-tank elements were not provided. The Combat Vehicles HQ and the 1st Battalion commanded by Major Stanimir Mišić were stationed in Belgrade. The 3 Companies of this armored unit, equipped with FT-17 and M-28 tanks, were then assigned to the 2nd Army in Sarajevo, to the 3rd Army in Skopje and to the 4th Army in Zagreb. The 2nd Battalion, located in Belgrade, conducted large-scale training maneuvers, in view of a potential combat employment. The Czechoslovak built T-32 light self-propelled guns serving with the Fast Combat Vehicle Squadron (Eskadron brzih borni kolah) were also involved in such military maneuvers. The Š-I-D or T-32 was the result of a specific Yugoslavian request. It was a vehicle developed in the mid-1930s by Škoda, based on the Š-I tankette (MU-4) with the addition of a simple fixed casemate to the original hull, armed with a modified version of the Škoda A3 37mm anti-tank gun. At the end of 1935, a prototype was shown to the Yugoslavian Ordnance Officers who, while appreciating the vehicle, submitted a number of suggestions for improvement, subsequently incorporated into the production version. The resultant vehicle was highly valued and in 1936 Yugoslavia signed a supply contract for 8 Š-I-Ds, subsequently accepted for service with the designation T-32. As we shall see, these light self-propelled guns had the opportunity to fight the Germans south of Belgrade. Very few T-32s fell into German hands. They were all sent to Škoda workshops for reconditioning. Intended for Waffen-SS units and used for training, the vehicle was designated Pz.Kpfw. T-32 732 (j)[6].

---

[3] The difference with the Yugoslavian Air Force was abysmal. The latter in fact had about 420 fighter planes, including modern aircraft such as Me Bf 109E-3, Hurricane Mk I and Ik-3 (built in Yugoslavia).
[4] It was an unidentified type of locally built armored car of the First World War.
[5] Some sources erroneously report that R-35s were assigned to the 1st Battalion. The reason for this incorrect identification lies in some photographs depicting a R-35 tank of the Royal Army showing a particular marking on its side toolbox, a grenade with a number 1. It was in fact a French marking, never covered with any paint.
[6] In 1937, the Yugoslavian government made some requests to Škoda engineers. In April 1938 the Czechoslovak company presented the prototype of a new larger model, Š-I-j ("j" stood for jugoslávský, Yugoslavian), with improved suspension system, new engine and enhanced armament. The vehicle was extensively tested in 1939-40, but the Yugoslavian Army decided to focus on heavier tanks, marking the end of the project. The prototype, brought back to Czechoslovakia, was finally taken by Waffen-SS on September 17, 1943 and sent to Munich to undergo new tests. Its fate is unknown, but it is known that vehicles of this type were still included in 1946 Škoda catalogue.

At the outbreak of fighting, the Royal Army was divided into 5 Corps, based in Novi Sad, Sarajevo, Skopje, Zagreb and Niš. They comprised 16 Infantry Divisions, 1 Separate Guards Division, 2 Cavalry Divisions, 32 Artillery Regiments, 6 Engineer Regiments, various services. In March 1941, the Yugoslavian government, formed thanks to the political agreement between the Serbian Dragiša Cvetković and the Croatian Vladimir Maček, was negotiating with the Germans to join the Axis powers. On March 25, Prime Minister Cvetković signed Yugoslavia's accession to the Tripartite Pact concluded by Italy, Germany and Japan, sealing the fate of the country. On March 27, 1941, only 36 hours after such decision, a part of the Yugoslavian armed forces put into practice a plot to overthrow the government. A group of Royal Air Force officers serving with units stationed in western Yugoslavia, led by General Dusan Simović, unleashed a coup d'état. In Belgrade the insurrection was also supported by the Army Garrison, which deployed the R-35 tanks of the 2nd Battalion commanded by Major Danilo Zobenica in key positions of the capital. The armored vehicles did not have to fire a single shot, but undoubtedly exerted a strong psychological impact. Some R-35s employed on that occasion displayed political slogans painted on the turret, for example "For the King and the Fatherland" ("За Краља и Отаџбину"). Within a few hours, the neutral and pro-Axis government was removed from power and the young Prince Peter was appointed King of Yugoslavia by the insurgents. That same day the accession to the Tripartite pact was denied and on April 5, Yugoslavia signed a non-aggression pact with Russia.

The new government, formed after the coup, became concerned about the possible reaction of Axis forces and began preparing for mobilization. At that time, the Kingdom of Yugoslavia had a numerically large Army on paper. According to the secret military mobilization plan of the Yugoslavian headquarters (code name "R 41"), about 1,2 million first-line troops and about 500,000 second-line troops could have been available in case of war. However, the whole process proved to be poorly organized and too slow, therefore fewer than 600,000 men were actually mobilized.

As a result of this sudden change of alliances, the Royal Army immediately sent numerous divisions to Italian and Albanian borders. In fact, a powerful Yugoslavian Army was deploying along the border with Albania, while on the border with Italy the situation appeared more calm. Adolf Hitler immediately reacted to the "betrayal" of the former ally and on the morning of April 6, 1941 launched operation "Unternehmen Strafgericht"[7], consisting of a massive bombing of Belgrade, causing the collapse of Yugoslavian high command. German diplomacy immediately urged the allied countries, Italy, Bulgaria and Hungary, to take part in the new conflict. On April 6, Italy commenced operations against Yugoslavia.

Elements of the 1st Combat Vehicle Battalion, under the orders of Major Stanimir Misić and equipped with the oldest tanks, were deployed to defend important cities such as Sarajevo and Zagreb. Most of the 2nd Battalion, now commanded by Captain Ljubisa Terzić, was instead positioned for the defense of Belgrade, with the exception of a Company[8] moved to Skopje as early as the fall of 1940. As soon as Axis forces attacked the Kingdom of Yugoslavia, the 2nd Battalion left Belgrade and moved to northern Croatia, in the hope of preventing any possible enemy advance. On April 9, the Battalion reached Đakovo in Dalmatia, where it was engaged against the Croatian rebellion aimed at disarming the Royal Army unit stationed in the city. The situation was rapidly deteriorating. The establishment of the Independent State

---

7 Also known as the "April War", it began the attack on Yugoslavia.
8 It probably was the 3rd Company.

of Croatia (Nezavisna Država Hrvatska - NDH) was proclaimed, with the support of the Germans, the following day, April 10, 1941. This event aggravated the confusion that reigned among the ranks of the Yugoslavian Royal Army stationed in Croatia, which was about to crumble due to the resistance opposed by rebel Croatian soldiers and the rapid progress of Axis troops. For this reason, some elements of the 2nd Battalion were quickly transferred to Bosnia, across the Sava River. On April 13, this small force reached Gračanica, to support Yugoslavian 2nd Army. The Supreme Command of the 2nd Army prescribed the formation of three motorized detachments, each equipped with 5 R-35 tanks, 5 trucks and assisted by infantry. These units were supposed to defend the area around Bosanska Posavina from Croatian rebels which were now openly attacking the Yugoslavian Royal Army. Because of the urgency, only one motorized department was formed, with no more than 3 or 4 R-35 tanks. The unit, named "2nd Army Fast Detachment", was commanded by General Dragoljub Draža Mihailović[9]. In the night between 13 and 14 April, the formation moved from Gračanica to its designated area. On the road to Bosanska Posavina, the Detachment ran into a large group of Croatian insurgent forces, defeated after a bloody fight, and minor German units, to which some losses were inflicted. The Fast Detachment, however, was destroyed near Sarajevo after being reached by Germans. Other units of the 2nd Battalion stationed in Bosnia were either destroyed or captured by the 14th Panzer Division.

The 2nd Battalion's Company located in Macedonia was perfectly fit for front-line service at the time of the Axis attack. On April 6 it was transferred to Ježevo Polje in support of the "Bregalnička" Division. The day after, Yugoslavian tanks helped repel a German attack before receiving orders to retreat to Veles in northern Macedonia. Nevertheless, owing to the heavy German offensive, all R35s were lost or abandoned by their crews during the retreat.

The same day Slavko Kvaternik, deputy leader of Ustaše, proclaimed the independence of Croatia, the 2nd Company of 1st Combat Vehicle Battalion surrendered without fighting in Zagreb. The Germans immediately seized the unit's armored vehicles, 16 old Renault FT-17 tanks. The 3rd Company of the 1st Battalion, deployed in Sarajevo, reached Aranđelovac area and then headed towards Orasac to protect withdrawing Yugoslavian formations. Contact with friendly forces, however, did not take place and the vehicles soon found themselves running out of fuel. The Company commander ordered to leave the tanks without opposing any resistance to the Germans. The 1st Company was the only unit of the 1st Battalion to engage the enemy on the battlefield. On the night of April 7, after having loaded men and vehicles on a train, the Company left Skopje for Strumičko Polje, where the unit was supposed to support the "Šumadija" Division. Around 1 pm, Yugoslavian crews spotted a column of the 1st Panzer SS Division "Leibstandarte SS Adolf Hitler". Any attempt to organize an effective resistance was however immediately precluded by a German air raid which destroyed most of the Yugoslavian light tanks, also attacked by enemy armored vehicles arrived on the spot later. Only 4 tanks, along with the remains of other Yugoslavian units, managed to cross the border with Greece in the following hours. They eventually ended up to be sabotaged by their crews. On April 6, 1941, the Fast Combat Vehicles Squadron, equipped with 8 T-32 light self-propelled guns, was at the Cavalry School at Zemun, north of Belgrade. The small armored unit was tasked to defend the local airport from enemy paratroopers and to counterattack possible

---

9 General Mihailović is famous because he later became the Commander of the Chetnik movement, the Serbian conservative and anti-communist resistance movement loyal to King Peter II. Chetniks were involved in a long and fierce civil war against the communist partisans led by Tito.

enemy penetrations towards the capital. Four days later, the Squadron, with the exception of a self-propelled gun under repair, was ordered to move south to attempt to reach Niš and join the units of the Yugoslavian 6th Army deployed in that sector, threatened by General von Kleist's 1. Panzergruppe. On 11 April, at dawn, after passing Topola, the Squadron set up to defend the road Mladenovać - Belgrade. Two armored vehicles left to explore in the direction of Kragujevać but with little luck, as both suffered mechanical failures: the first was abandoned by the crew without having made contact with the enemy, the second came out unscathed from a brief clash with a German armored column before being immobilized. The remaining T-32s tried in vain to stop the advance of the Panzers. The Squadron commander, Major Dušan Radovic, managed to damage some German armored vehicles but was killed while trying to leave his self-propelled gun, now bursting into flames. The war ended on April 17, 1941 with the Yugoslavian capitulation, followed by the occupation and division of the territory by Axis forces: the Royal Family and some members of the government went into exile in Great Britain. All tanks of the Yugoslavian Royal Army were used and lost (at least thirty completely destroyed, the others captured by the enemy) during the "April War". Several units simply surrendered, others, as we have seen, tried to resist the Italian-German attack with little success or left Yugoslavia, seeking shelter in Greece. Overall, the armored forces of the Yugoslavian Royal Army turned out to be too small for a modern war, strategically unprepared and technically inferior to the Axis forces. The Germans captured at least 78-80 tanks and, at the end of June 1941, some, mainly R-35s, were used to form the Panzer Kompanie z.b.V .12, a unit engaged in the fight against the resistance movement in Yugoslavia.

Colors of Yugoslavian armored fighting vehicles

The FT-17, M-28 and R-35 tanks of the Yugoslavian Royal Army retained the French dark green color, although a limited number of FT-17s and M-28s had a camouflage scheme. The FT-17s showed the original French white numbers ranging from 66000 to 74000 on the front plate and left hull side. The M-28s carried two-digit numbers between 81 and 88, always painted on the front or left side. The first R-35s delivered to Yugoslavia maintained on front and rear plates their original French registration four-digit numbers, ranging from 49XX to 50XX, in white. In addition, various R-35s exhibited patriotic slogans on the turret during the coup d'état of March 27, 1941. The presence of a symbol depicting a grenade with the number 1 on the toolboxes positioned on the hull sides of some R-35s of the Royal Army, led to the hypothesis that these vehicles were assigned to the 1st Combat Vehicles Battalion. It was a actually a French emblem, which was never covered or repainted, typical of the units originally equipped with these tanks.
The Škoda Š-I-D tankettes (T-32) sported the mottled camouflage used by the Czechoslovak Army, characterized by sharp edges, with dark brown, dark green and ochre spots and had no specific identification markings.

▲ A Yugoslavian tank crew aboard a Renault FT-17. This photograph was taken in late 1920s.

▲ Two Automitrailleuse White M1918 armored cars serving with an unidentified Yugoslavian armored unit are shown here parading in front of military authorities. This picture probably dates back to the early 1930s.

▼ Another image of the same parade, showing Renault-Kegresse M-28 tanks of the Yugoslavian Royal Army.

▲ A Yugoslavian M-28. Tanks of this type exclusively equipped the 1st Combat Vehicle Battalion.

▼ King Peter II of Yugoslavia personally tests the first French R-35 tank delivered to the Yugoslavian Royal Army.

▲ Peter II, the very young ruler of Yugoslavia, inspects a Renault R-35 tank.

▼ Front view of a Renault R-35 employed by the Yugoslavian Royal Army. This tank is painted with French dark green overall.

▲ A modern Czechoslovak T-32 tankette (also known as Š-I-D) pictured during a parade held in 1940. This photograph allows to appreciate the typical Czechoslovak camouflage of the vehicle.

▼ A rare shot showing a T-32 commander: the photograph makes you appreciate the uniform and the French manufactured tanker helmet used by Yugoslavian crews.

▲ Rear view of a Škoda T-32 tankette (Authors' archive).

▼ Soldiers from the Belgrade Army Garrison, being supported by a Renault R-35 tank from the 2nd Battalion, in the streets of the Yugoslavian capital during the coup d'état of March 27, 1941.

▲ Another shot depicting the streets of Belgrade during the insurrection. An antiaircraft gun position is visible on the right in the picture.

▼ A Renault R-35 tank of the 2nd Battalion on Ulica Kneza Miloša (Prince Michael Street) pictured during the anti-government insurrection of March 27, 1941. Mihailo Obrenović III of Serbia, governor of Serbia, managed to definitively expel the Turks from the country, by means of a careful diplomatic activity, in 1867.

▲ Another Renault R-35 near Ulica Kneza Miloša. The political slogan painted on the turret reads: "For the King and the Fatherland".

▼ A Renault R-35 of the 2nd Battalion photographed in Belgrade on March 27, 1941. The presence of a French insignia, consisting of a flaming grenade with the number 1 painted on the right side of the upper hull, is of interest.

▲ A Renault-Kegresse M-28 and a FT-17 destroyed and abandoned during the "April war" (B.A.).

▼ Another Renault-Kegresse M-28 abandoned after fierce fighting against the overwhelming invading German forces.

▲ Many Yugoslavian tanks were left intact by their crews, afraid of the swift German advance. For this reason, most of Yugoslavian armored vehicles were captured by German troops.

▼ One of the R-35s assigned to the "2nd Army Fast Detachment" knocked out in a Yugoslavian town during the "April War".

▲ A Renault R-35 abandoned in northern Bosnia. The French registration number, 5009, is clearly visible on the right front hull.

▼ A German motorized column passing a Yugoslavian Š-I-D tankette lying along a country road. This self-propelled gun was left intact by the crew. The T-32 proved to be a sufficiently modern and well-armed vehicle but due to the limited number of units produced by Czechoslovakia and consequently employed by Yugoslavia, its qualities were never fully appreciated.

▲ Another abandoned T-32. The tankette's right track had been hit.

▼ Three-quarter rear view of a Š-I-D tankette lying on a field after a confrontation with the Germans.

▲ A T-32 light self-propelled gun abandoned after suffering damage to the left track.

▼ The self-propelled gun of the previous picture is shown here surrounded by German soldiers.

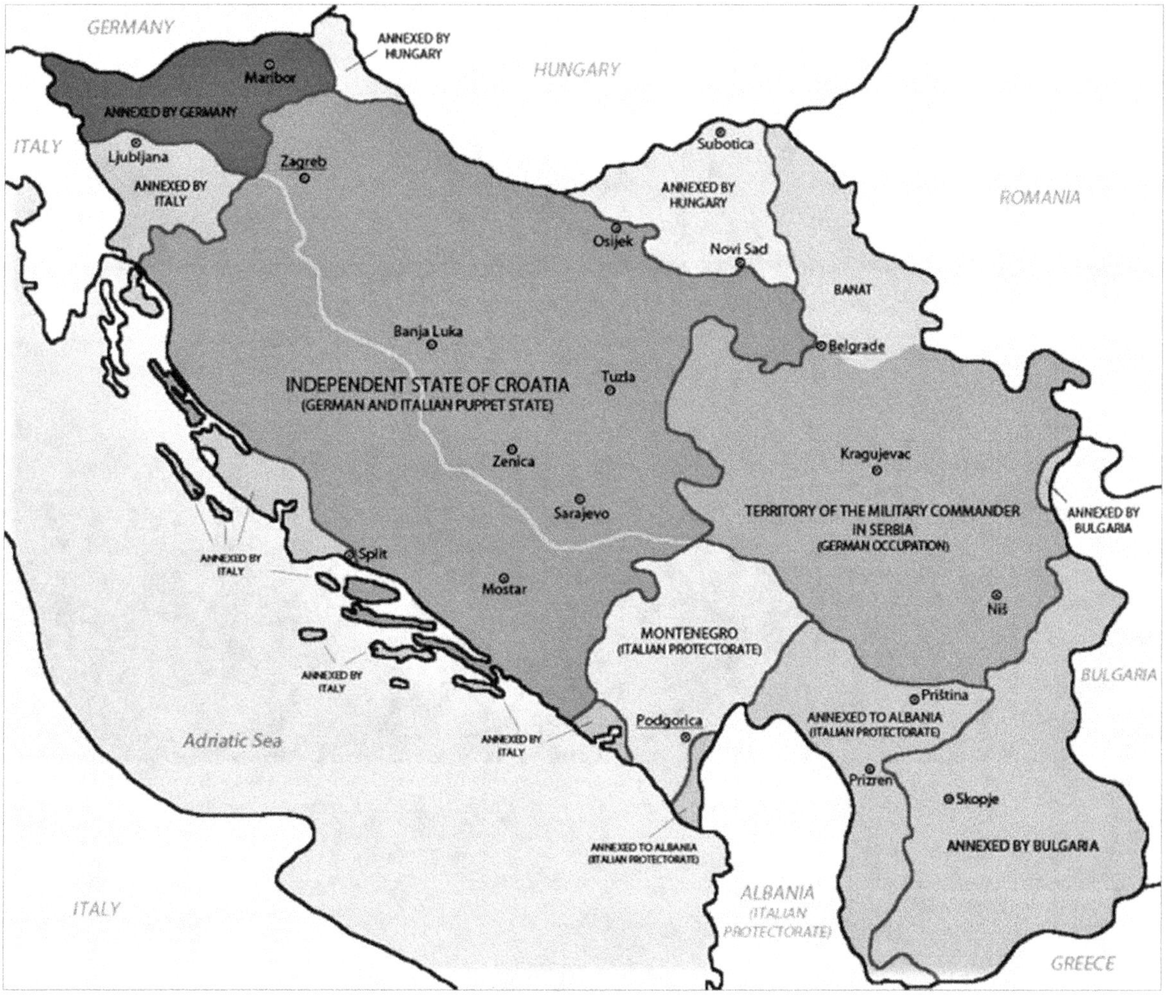

▲ An interesting map showing the division of the Yugoslavian territory between the Kingdom of Italy, the Reich, Hungary, the Independent State of Croatia and Bulgaria.

▼ This White M1918 armored car was destroyed near Mladenovac, a town located about 60 km south of Belgrade.

▲ In addition to the Fast Combat Vehicles Squadron, a platoon consisting of three armored cars was also stationed in Zemun on the eve of the Axis offensive. The vehicle depicted here, a Berliet-White M1918, had presumably fallen into German hands south of Belgrade.

▼ Tanks in good condition captured by the Germans, such as the M-28 portrayed in this image, underwent several tests.

▲ Yugoslavian FT-17 light tanks captured by the Germans. The vehicle in the foreground is equipped with an octagonal turret made up of riveted plates, armed with the classic 37 mm Puteaux SA 18 gun.

▼ The Š-I-D tankettes captured by the Germans were reused by the Wehrmacht with the official designation of Pz.Kpfw 732 (j) after the annihilation of the Yugoslavian Army. As demonstrated in this photograph taken in Topola (Serbia), the vehicles were repainted in panzergrey and received German crosses as an identifying symbol.

▲ The Yugoslavian campaign earned a fair amount of tanks to the Germans, including the Renault FT-17 shown in this photograph.

▲ An abandoned Renault R-35 in northern Bosnia. On the front plate of the vehicle stands out, on the right, the French registration number: 5009.

▼ Two German motorcyclists are immortalized on a captured T-32 tankette.

▲ A German motorcyclist stops in front of the tankette of the previous picture.

▼ The characteristic Czechoslovakian camouflage, with three tones and sharp edges, stands out clearly on these two self-propelled light Š-I-D photograpghed in 1938.

▲ Two light T-32 self-propelled T-32s photographed before the outbreak of war.

▼ A column of light self-propelled Š-I-D. These are vehicles portrayed during an exercise held before the war.

▲ A T-32 tankette captured by the Germans in Serbia in 1941.

▼ Elements of the 11th Panzer Division cross the remains of a Yugoslavian motorized column near Topola on December 11, 1941.

▲ Three Yugoslav military men pose with an FT-17 light wagon. The photograph probably dates back to the early 1930s.

▼ A Yugoslav M-28. Wagons of this type were exclusively assigned to 1st Battalion Combat Vehicles.

▲ A Renault M-28 wagon, individual number 81, parades along a street in Belgrade. The main armament of the tank consists of an 8 mm Hotchkiss machine gun.

▼ M-28 wagons on parade. The original description of this photograph is dated 27 March 1941, the day of the coup that brought Prince Peter to the throne of Yugoslavia. However, it cannot be excluded that the shot dates back to the early 1930s (US NARA).

▲ Another Yugoslav M-28 light wagon abandoned by its crew.

▼ A Renault-Kegresse M-28 probably destroyed the day after the start of Operation "Unternehmen 25", the invasion of Yugoslavia (B.A.).

ŠKODA T-32
SQUADRONE CELERE VEICOLI DA COMBATTIMENTO
ESERCITO REALE JUGOSLAVO 1941

RENAULT R-35
2° BATTAGLIONE
BELGRADO 27 MARZO 1941

PANZER I AUSF A
DELLA GUARDIA NAZIONALE CROATA 1942

HOTCHKISS H39
DI UNA BRIGATA USTAŠA 1943

CARRO LEGGERO L3/33
DI UNA BRIGATA USTAŠA
SECONDA METÀ DEL 1944

SEMOVENTE DA 47/32 L40
DEI DOMOBRANCI SLOVENI
SECONDA METÀ DEL 1944

© Paolo Paolino Crippa 2020

▲ Profiles of Yugoslav, Croatian and Slovenian armoured vehicles (original drawing by Paolo Crippa)

CROATIAN ARMORED UNITS

On April 10, 1941, four days after the German invasion of Yugoslavia, Croatia became an independent state, ruled by a government led by Ante Pavelić, head of the pro-fascist political-military organization of the Ustaša. A veritable emissary of the dictates of the German Reich, animated by an anti-Yugoslavian spirit, Pavelić planned a severe ethnic cleansing in the country, directed above all against the Serbs, regarded as the real enemies of Croatia, the Jews and the Gypsies. The Independent State of Croatia (Nezavisna Drzava Hrvatska - NDH) included part of present-day Croatia and the whole territory of Bosnia and Herzegovina. In formal terms it was a monarchy and an Italian protectorate, headed by Prince Aimone of Savoy - Aosta, who never set foot on Croatian soil, thus leaving the country in the hands of Pavelić. In reality, the Croatian territory was occupied by both Italian and German Armed Forces, while Dalmatia was annexed to the Kingdom of Italy. Croatia, obviously an ally of Germany and Italy, quickly organized its Armed Forces: the day after the declaration of independence, the Croatian National Guard (Hrvastko Domobranstvo), dependent on the Ministry of Defense, was created. On April 16, the real Armed Forces were organized, consisting of the Army (Kopnena Vojska), the Air Force (Zrakoplovstvo Nezavisne Drzave Hrvatske) and the Gendarmerie (Hrvastko Oružništvo). However, the Ustaša found themselves taking on a prominent paramilitary formation position, very similar, in Pavelić's intentions, to the Waffen SS. The vastness and nature of the Croatian territory, mainly mountainous, and the need to hold off Tito's partisans and Mihailovic's Chetniks were the reasons that led the military authorities to organize armored support units for the infantry, asking for armored vehicles to Germany and to Italy. On July 1, by the order of the Ground Force Command, all members of the dissolved armored units were assigned to the 1st Mobile Battalion of Zagreb (1. Automobilskog Batalijuna Domobranstva), for the reconstitution of tank units, but the equipment situation turned out to be dramatic, because armored vehicles were missing. The government had in fact tried to seize tanks of the dissolved Royal Yugoslavian Army, but most of these vehicles were requisitioned by the occupying German forces, with the exception of some Renault FT-17s and R-35s. In late spring 1941, Germany supplied the Ustaša with a number of tanks of low value (Polish tankettes and old Renault FT-17s, the latter previously belonging to the Yugoslavian Royal Army) and, only in December, 4 Panzer Is for the Croatian National Guard. Croatia obtained 15 L3 tanks from the fascist regime, to equip its armored units; in October of that year an Armored Company belonging to the Guards Battalion Poglavnikova Tjelesna Bojna (P.T.B.) was formed in Zagreb; "Poglavnik" was the title with which Pavelić was indicated, a name that, translated into Italian, sounds like "leader", a clear reference to the fascist "Duce" and the Nazi "Führer". The Company, which actually was the first armored unit of independent Croatia, was initially equipped with 6 Italian L3/33 light tanks and 4 Polish TK-3 tankettes; during the course of the conflict this unit was heavily engaged in anti-partisan repression.

At first, owing to various training readiness problems and lack of suitable vehicles, the armored units were only used for convoy escort duties. Nonetheless they began to be employed in anti-partisan operations as early as December 1941.

At the beginning of 1942, the Croatian General Staff decided to increase the offensive potential of the Ustaša, joining an armored company equipped with 2/6 Italian light tanks to each of the first 5 Ustaša Brigades; in the same period, 4 Mountain Brigades and 4 Jäger Brigades of the Croatian National Guard were also being raised. Each of these Brigades should have had a Tank Platoon consisting of 3 medium tanks and 2 light tanks. According to a British secret report, the Croatian Army had 12 Renault FT-17 tanks, used on armed trains in the middle of 1942; the same report also mentions that Croatians had obtained from the German Armed Forces the promise to receive 21 5-ton tanks, probably all Czechoslovak LT-34s, to be destined for the 3rd Corps operations in Bosnia. These tanks were actually never delivered, since they were practically unusable. Between 1942 and 1943 (sources disagree on the actual date) Hungary also supplied various armored vehicles to Croatia, sending a batch of 10 L3/33 light tanks (some with a modified commander's cupola); these vehicles merged into a single armored battalion along with the Italian ones already present. The available tanks were often sent to areas where the intervention of small armored detachments was needed, acting independently in temporary support of friendly units engaged in the anti-partisan struggle.

Starting from 1943, the Ustaša further increased their armament and potential offensive capabilities to the detriment of the regular Army. Overall, at that time, Croatia had about 40 light tanks, mainly Italian L3s and Polish TK-3 and TKF tankettes (the TKF version was reconditioned with a Fiat 122BC engine, produced under license in Poland). Given the variety of vehicles available, the Armored Troops Command, dependent on the Ministry of Defense, was established in Zagreb on 1st July 1943; its task was the supply and maintenance of armored vehicles, as well as crew training. This Command, sometimes also referred to as Armored Companies Command, was supposed to coordinate the Armored Companies formed for the Jäger and Mountain Brigades. As we have seen, the aim was to form 8 armored platoons, with 5 tanks each, between Panzer Is, TK-3s, TKFs and other types of tanks supplied by the Germans[10].

With the capitulation of Italy, the Croatians managed to grab 26 L6/40 light tanks and an unknown number of 47/32 L40 self-propelled guns, lying in Italian depots of the Dalmatian coast; a dozen L6/40s were captured by the Ustaša in the areas of Jastrebarsko and Karlovac; the Germans supplied the Croatians with other equipment, giving 13 Italian L3 tanks to the 4th Ustaša Brigade in December 1943; according to a German secret report, the Croatians also had some Pz.Kpfw. I Ausf. As at that time[11]. Photographic evidence allows us to assert that Pavelić's militia also had AB41 armored cars and FIAT 666 NM shielded trucks, although these vehicles were not mentioned in official documents. In the meantime (October 1943), the Ustaša armored forces were grouped in a Fast Brigade, "Brzi Ustaski Zdrug", based in Travnik, which had a nominal strength of 2 Tank Battalions and 2 Motorized Battalions. Since the end of 1943, the Ustaša armored units were mainly used in three areas: south-west and north of Zagreb (Zagoje) and in the Gospic sector .

---

10 Some sources even mention a German program to reinforce all the Hrvastko Domobranstvo Brigades under creation with an armored platoon equipped with Panzer IIs and Panzer IIIs. Obviously, this program remained on paper.
11 Some Croatian crews were transferred to the Reich and trained on Panzer IV tanks. Partisan sources, moreover, seem to confirm the use of at least one heavier tank than those used by the Croatians in Sernya by the Ustaša (perhaps a Panzer IV). Other sources even cite a delivery consisting of 20 Pz.Kpfw III Ausf. Ns, 10 Pz.Kpfw IV Ausf. Fs and 5 Pz.Kpfw IV Ausf. Hs to the P.T.D. in the autumn of 1944. These tanks allegedly took part in battles against Red Army and Bulgarian Army in Croatia in 1945.

At the beginning of 1944, Mountain Brigades and Jäger Brigades were equipped with Italian L3 tanks, Polish TK-3 tankettes and French Hotchkiss H39 tanks (10/12 captured H39s were supplied by the Germans)[12]. In the spring of 1944 the Germans provided 4 Italian L40 self-propelled guns to equip the Pavelić Guard Artillery Regiment. Armored detachments of the P.T.B. took part in the anti-partisan Operation Rouen on the Kalnik Mountains, north-east of Zagreb, in July 1944. In November 1944, Ante Pavelić decided to merge the Army and Ustaša Vojnica, which now held the record in terms of military potential, into a single armed force, the Hrvastke Oruzane Snege, whereas the Poglavnik Guard was to remain independent. The Army Mobile Regiment merged into the Poglavnik Guard Armored Company, which increasingly took the form of a mechanized Division, becoming the Poglavnikova Tjelesna Divjzia (P.T.D.) in January 1945. The armored units of the Army, for their parts, merged into the so-called "Elite Divisions" (Hrvatska Udarna Divizja), which were employed south-west and north-east of Zagreb. According to some post-war sources, in this period Germany sold to Croatia between 20 and 25 Pz.Kpfw. III Ausf. Ns, 10 Pz.Kpfw. IV Ausf. Fs, 5 Pz.Kpfw. IV Ausf. Gs tanks and 15 Hanomag Sd.Kfz 251 armored half-tracks; the crews of these vehicles were composed of Ustaša tankmen trained by German instructors[13].

At the end of 1944, the Croatian Armed Forces had a total of 85 armored vehicles distributed as follows:

- P.T.B. = 35 vehicles
- Ustaša Brigades = 26 vehicles
- Mountain Brigades = 9 vehicles
- Reserve Brigades = 7 vehicles
- Mobile Brigade (Brzi Zdrug) = 5 vehicles
- Various units = 3 vehicles

As we can see, the Jäger Brigades hadn't armored vehicles at that time; as we will see later, the armored platoons of these Brigades were in fact dissolved at the end of 1944. Although not mentioned in official papers, some evidence suggests that, in January 1945, a few Croatian tanks (presumably Pz.Kpfw. IVs obtained from the Germans a few months earlier or, more likely, tanks belonging to one of the three German Infantry Divisions) were sent to Syrmia to fight against Soviet and Bulgarian forces. The first months of 1945 saw the increasing pressure of Tito's partisans and, consequently, Croatian armored units were expected to be heavily committed to battles. In early May, Pavelić ordered that the bulk of the Croatian Armed Forces concentrated in Zagreb; the order was to move to Austria, to escape from partisans. Besides the P.T.B. tanks, a number of serviceable armored vehicles, previously under repair, were also put into action, in order to ensure the necessary protection to the withdrawing forces. Fighting their way, the Croatians reached the Austrian border on May 14, when the last clashes took place. The survivors were concentrated in the British prisoner of war camp of Grafenstein, near Klagenfurt. Many of them were later picked up by Yugoslavian partisans.

---

12 Statement by Podpukovnik (Lieutenant Colonel) Ivan Babic, given to allied intelligence during an interrogation after his desertion.

13 There are photographs of Pz.Kpf. IVs with Croatian markings but, presumably, these tanks belonged to the 3 German Wehrmacht Divisions using Croatian soldiers.

These prisoners began a dramatic march to Ljubljana, during which they were subjected to atrocities such that this long journey was later called "Via Crucis". Many officers were executed, the worst fate fell to the Ustaša (frowned upon by the majority of Croatian population) and many of their families.

Croatian units

Below is a summary of information about Croatian armored units, mentioned in official documents.

Tank Company of the 1ˢᵗ Ustaša Brigade
As of December 1941, it was equipped with an unspecified number of Italian CV33 tanks. In autumn 1942 it was located in Sarajevo and handed over 2 tanks to the 5th Ustaša Brigade. The unit took part with 6 light tanks in the Operation "Jajce I". At the end of 1944, with only 3 remaining tanks, it was reduced into a single platoon.

Tank Company of the 3ʳᵈ Ustaša Brigade
What is known is that this unit was formed with 7 tanks in early 1944.

Tank Company of the 4ᵗʰ Ustaša Brigade[14]
Named 3rd P.T.B Tank Company, this unit was formed in Gospic in August 1942. As of October 15, 1943, it could count on 7 L3 tanks[15] and consisted of 2 officers, 5 non-commissioned officers and 32 enlisted men. The Company was commanded by Ustaša Nadporučnik (Lieutenant of the Ustaša) Ivan Milardović. Between March and June 1943 it was engaged in heavy fighting against the partisans. A Yugoslavian Resistance report, dated 11 June 1943, indicates that the unit was equipped with 10 Italian L3 tanks, only 6 operational. In the spring of 1944, the Company was included in a order of a battle with a strength of 7 L3 tanks and 39 motorized vehicles of various types; in July, a document reported that the unit, with its 15 light tanks, was assigned to the 4th Ustaša Brigade, located in Gospic. This Company was still operating with 8 CV33 tanks at the end of 1944.

Tank Company of the 5ᵗʰ Ustaša Brigade
This Company was initially established in May 1942, using 2/3 armored trucks with improvised armor, called "Oklopni Samozov", due to the lack of armored vehicles. Active in eastern Herzegovina and central Bosnia, the unit received 2 L3 tanks from the 1st Brigade at the end of 1942; the Company was based in Livno and had 1 officer, 3 non-commissioned officers and 48 men. One of the armored trucks was captured by the Yugoslavian partisans, and used against the Kupres garrison in December 1942; the truck was recaptured by the Ustaša during those fights. In January 1944, the unit acted south of Sarajevo, probably assigned to the 1st Ustaša Brigade.

---

14 Reported in some documents as 3rd P.T.S. Carriage Company.
15 Oddly reported as tanks armed with a single weapon in official documentation.

Tank Companies of the P.T.B.

A P.T.B. tank company was first mentioned on December 8, 1941, when it participated with its tanks[16] in a parade held in Zagreb, assigned to the Motorized Group (Brzi Sklop) of the Poglavnik Guard. This unit was involved in a vast operation against the insurgency in the Kordun area, as well as in various anti-partisan operations, with 6 CV35 tanks, in January 1942; during the following six months, the Company was equipped with only 5 CV35 tanks. In August 1942, the unit was reorganized and divided into the 1st and 2nd Tank Company, due to the fact that it had probably received reinforcement vehicles (Hungary sold to Croatia 10 L3 tanks in that period), both based in Zagreb. At the same time, the 3rd Tank Company, was also assigned to the P.T.B. and was located in Gospic along with the 4th Brigade. Reports concerning the following months always indicate for both companies a strength of 10 L3 tanks (all CV35s) engaged in anti-partisan operations. In early 1943, the Ustaša and the National Guard conducted various operations in the Zumberak area to regain control of the region; the support provided by the two Armored Companies of the P.T.B., notably in clearing roads and railways between Karlovac and Zagreb, was fundamental. In the spring of 1943, the companies operated first in Slavonia and then in the Varazdin area, with 12 L3s altogether. In August, the 1st Company was stationed in Zagreb and the 2nd in Krapina; the number of serviceable armored vehicles had risen to 20 by the end of the year, probably thanks to the L3 and L6 tanks captured after the Italian armistice. In 1944, both companies were again concentrated in Zagreb, under the control of the Motorized Group, and amalgamated into a single unit, the Armored Group; in April, the Group, equipped with 20 L3s and an unknown number of L6/40s, was put under the P.T.B. command. After being heavily engaged in actions against Tito's partisans throughout the spring, the Armored Group was reorganized as follows:

- 1st Medium Tank Company (with a strength of 15 tanks);
- 2nd Light Tank Company (with a strength of 7 tanks)[17];
- 3rd Motorized Infantry Company;
- 4th Motorized Infantry Company;
- 5th Company Command with Engineer, Signals, Anti-tank and Maintenance platoons.

At that time, the P.T.B. Motorized Group still had the 3rd Tank Company, assigned to the 4th Ustaša Brigade with a strength of 15 light tanks in Gospic. In October, both the Armored Group and the Motorized Group took part in the defense of the city of Koprivnica, besieged by the partisans, losing 6 armored vehicles. At the end of the year, the Armored Group had two companies, each with 10 tanks, while the Motorized Group had a company equipped with 8 tanks. Before the end of the war there was time for further reorganization: the Poglavnikov Tjelesni Sdruga (P.T.S. or Poglavnik Guard Corps) was established in the first days of April 1945. The P.T.S. was made up of the P.T.D. (Poglavnikova Tjelesna Divjzia), the 1st Croatian Elite Division (Hrvatska Udarna Divizja or H.U.D.) and the 5th Croatian Elite Division.

---

16 Some sources mention that the Company probably had Polish TK-3 tankettes; this is in contrast with what is reported in some documents issued after the parade which, as to the following lines, always mention Italian light tanks.
17 A document, dated 15 June, reported that P.T.D. had 26 L6/40s, of which only 4 serviceable, due to the lack of spare parts. The P.T.D. was awaiting delivery of the necessary spare parts from the German authorities.

The P.T.D. had the Armored Group, divided into two Companies[18], and a Motorized Group; the 1st Division had its own Motorized Group. In the first days of May 1944, the Poglavnik ordered to concentrate all the available tanks in Zagreb, to try to organize an orderly retreat to Austria. The tanks, not only coming from the Armored Group of the P.T.D., but probably from other several units, were supposed to cover the movements of the Free Croatia Armed Forces. Undergoing heavy fighting, the surviving units with still about thirty serviceable tanks reached the Austrian border on 14 May. Last losses were recorded that day: 3 tanks were destroyed by bazooka rounds during a clash with the 8th Partisan Brigade south of Dravograd.

Ustaša Obrana (Ustaša Defense Unit)
Created in 1942 and directly dependent on the Ministry of the Interior, the Ustaša Obrana was a rapid intervention unit, engaged in various areas of Croatia. Placed under the Ustaša Brigade from 1944, it had an Armored Company equipped with all variants of L3s, L6/40 light tanks and at least one M15/42 tank provided with a Pz.Kpfw. 38 (t) turret.

1st Light Tank Company of the 1st Mountain Division
Commanded by Natporučnik (Lieutenant) Subotić, it was involved in operations conducted in Hercegovac, Palesnik and Virovitica areas in February 1943, before being moved southwest of Virovitica later that month. It was equipped with 14 French light tanks, 7 of which non-operational. On April 7, a 5-tank platoon took part in Operation "Braun", during which 2 tanks were damaged by enemy fire. In August 1943, when the Division was disbanded, the Company's personnel and equipment were distributed to the 1st and 4th Mountain Brigades.

Tank Platoon of the 1st Mountain Brigade
It was established with the remnants of the Tank Company of the 1st Mountain Division in August 1943. The platoon had 5 armored vehicles: 3 French Somua tanks and 2, probably Italian built, light tanks. This unit was still operational at the end of 1944.

Tank Platoon of the 3rd Mountain Brigade
It was equipped with 3 Hotchkiss H39 tanks and was stationed in Banja Luka in September 1944.

Tank Platoon of the 4th Mountain Brigade
The platoon, equipped with 5 tanks, was set up with the remnants of the 1st Light Tank Company of the 1st Mountain Division, in the middle of August 1943. Between April 24 and May 8, 1944, this small unit participated in the "Ungerwitter" operation in the Papuk Mountains. It was still active with 3 Somua S35 tanks in December of that year.

Tank platoon of the 3rd Jäger Brigade
Included in an order of battle dated August 15, 1944, it was disbanded in December of that year.

---

18 At that time only equipped with Italian armored vehicles, 11 L6/40 tanks and 4 47/32 L40 self-propelled guns.

Tank Platoon of the 4th Jäger Brigade

Equipped with 4 Somua or Hotchkiss medium tanks, the unit was mentioned in a order of battle dated June 1, 1944. It was dissolved in December of the same year.

Light Tank Company

It was established in the spring of 1942, as part of the Croatian army. It was initially equipped with 4 Panzer Is received from Germany in late 1941 and 16 TK-3s, added in May of the following year. Stationed in Daruvan, the Company handed over some vehicles to the 3rd Corps Tank Platoon when it was transferred to Sarajevo. The formation was engaged in clashes against the partisans in Slavonia, Bosnia and Herzegovina, until the end of 1942. It was reorganized into the 1st Armored Company and Armored Reserve Company in March 1943.

Armored Reserve Company (also referred to as Armored Reserve Command)

It was formed thanks to the reorganization of the Light Tank Company in March 1943. There are reports of the Armored Reserve Company dating back to September 1943, when the unit was deployed in Zagreb with a strength of 3 medium tanks and 3 light tanks, employed by the 1st Reserve Brigade. At the beginning of the following year, the Company was equipped with 7 unspecified tanks.

3rd Corps Tank Platoon

The Platoon was established as an independent unit, with a strength of 41 men and 6/9 Polish tankettes, at the end of November 1941. On May 28, 1942, it was transferred to Sarajevo. On June 15, 1942, 2 tanks were sent by train from Sarajevo to Zepce. These vehicles took part in some actions around Vlasenica and were disabled by enemy fire the next day. Nothing is known of subsequent actions, except that 3 tanks provided support to the 1st Battalion of the 5th Infantry Regiment, south of Sarajevo, on July 4, 1942.

Light Tank Platoon of the 1st Transport Battalion

On February 1, 1943 the formation had 5 light tanks and was located in Zagreb. On 17 February the Platoon was transferred to Glina, employed by a larger unit, and in June of the same year it was assigned to the 5th Mountain Brigade. By the spring of 1944, after being presumably amalgamated into the Tank Company of the 3rd Ustaša Brigade, it was no longer mentioned in Croatian order of battles.

"Oklopni Samovoz" improvised armored fighting vehicles

These curious armored trucks, which had a strictly local use, deserved a particular mention. Starting from the clashes in Eastern Herzegovina in May 1942, the Croatian Armed Forces used armored trucks called "Oklopni Samovoz". Produced in an unspecified number, these armored cars were normal transport trucks, about 8 meters long, on which a special armor, probably taken from a factory located in the region (the workshops of the mines of Ljubija or the "Ferrosilicum" industrial plants in Jajce) had been applied. These vehicles were capable to transport, in addition to the crew, about fifteen soldiers, who could fire from appropriate slits on the side shields. "Oklopni Samovoz" armored trucks also had a revolving turret armed with a machine gun, sporting the Ustaša coat of arms. Therefore, these vehicles were almost certainly an exclusive prerogative of Pavelić's militia.

"Samovoz" trucks took part in various fights occurred in Jajce area in June and were often targeted by partisans, especially when carrying out escort duties. One of these armored trucks was used as a permanent escort vehicle for the column led by Colonel Simic, commander of Ustaša and Domobranci forces in the vicinities of Pliva and Rama. The column fell into an ambush by Tito's partisans near the village of Jezera on June 8, 1942, but succeded to disengage losing only one soldier. On the night of August 10, one of these armored trucks, operating as a fire support vehicle, took part in the defense of the city of Kupres, hit by a fierce partisan attack. Although the first attempt to conquer the town was foiled, it was repeated 3 days later: in fact, on the night of June 13, the partisans tried again to break into Kupres but the "Samovoz" assisted every counterattack brought by the Ustaša. The armored vehicle, which opened gaps in the enemy ranks, was attacked and damaged by small groups armed with hand grenades several times, but wasn't disabled.

A "Samovoz", deployed in Jajce, was captured by Resistance fighters on September 24. The partisans employed this armored truck in the following months, losing it, in turn, during an attack conducted on Kupres on December 28.

Colors of Croatian armored fighting vehicles

The TK-3 tankettes retained their original shade, with the only additions of a skull with crossbones painted in white on the superstructure front and the Croatian shield on the casemate sides. Armored vehicles of French origin, like Renault and Hotchkiss tanks, maintained a sand yellow color, probably applied by previous owners (the Germans); the Pz.Kpfw. Is had the usual "panzer" grey color and showed the Croatian shield on the hull sides. The Croatians employed all variants of L3 tanks: L3/33s, L3/35s and L3/38s. Both Italian and Hungarian L3 light tanks, seem painted in a uniform dark color; it can therefore be assumed that they were painted in the standard dark green color; tanks of the Ustaša Brigades sported on the glacis plate the characteristic emblem of this paramilitary formation, a large white U, which contained the red and white chequer-board shield (with 25 red and white squares) of Croatia. Italian built L6 light tanks seem painted in the usual three-tone camouflage scheme typical of Ansaldo production, consisting of a sand yellow base color with red brown and green spots; initially these vehicles did not show any identification sign, on the contrary, in some cases they even kept their original Italian plates. In 1944 the Croatian state's crest was painted on the four sides of the hull, while, according to photographic evidence, this crest was moved to the sides of the turret in the last months of the war, while the emblem of Pavelić's militia was present on the hull front. AB41 armored cars appear to have been camouflaged in the classic three-color scheme (brown and green spots on a sand yellow background), while, according to the rare and bad quality images found, FIAT 665 NM shielded trucks showed a single color, presumably a sand yellow factory applied paint. The coat of arms of the Croatian state was painted on the front and on the body of the shielded trucks, whereas AB41s had it on the hull sides along with the Ustaša insignia on the casemate front and rear. Available pictures show the use of plates painted in large letters and white numbers on the tanks of the Ustaška Obrana: for example, one CV38 tank had the plate "UO 123", three L6/40 tanks had plates "UO 128", "UO 129" and "UO 130" respectively, while a M15/42 equipped with the turret of a Pz.Kpfw. 38 (t) had the plate "UO 139".

▲ Ante Pavelić, head of the Independent State of Croatia (Nezavisna Drzava Hrvatska - NDH), chairs a parliamentary session. The soldier behind him holds the "Poglavnik" standard. Pavelić assumed the position of "Poglavnik" ("leader"), a title which clearly referred to the Italian "Duce" and the German "Führer".

▲ Detail of the Poglavnik's standard.

▼ A Polish built TK-3 tankette used by Croatian Armed Forces. The skull and crossbones symbol painted on the superstructure at the front and the Croatian shield emblem applied on the sides are certainly of interest.

▲ A TK-3 tankette passes some German soldiers during a mopping-up operation. The TK-3 was called the "Ursus" by Croatians.

▼ A TK-3 tankette, belonging to Croatian National Guard, supporting soldiers from the 1st Battalion of Einsatzstaffel Prinz Eugen in 1942.

▲ Italian built tanks used by Croatians firstly paraded in Zagreb on December 5 1941. All vehicles portrayed here are Italian CV33s serving with Ustaša P.T.S. Note the use of Italian tanker protective clothing.

▼ Ustaša L3/35 Italian built tank, during the swearing-in ceremony of Ustaša cadets in Zagreb; an Italian machine gun FIAT 35 sat on its tripod next to the armored vehicle (HPM).

▲ Another image from the same ceremony. Two L3/35 tanks are seen in the middle of the picture (HPM).

▼ Panzer I Ausf A of the Croatian National Guard in winter: the Croatian state's crest (HDA) was painted over the original German hue.

▲ A Tank Platoon of the Croatian National Guard, consisting of 3 Panzer Is and a Renault R-35, photographed in the vicinities of Zagreb, Croatia's capital city.

▼ Side view of a Panzer I Ausf A serving with the Croatian National Guard.

▲ Men of the Croatian National Guard. A Renault FT-17 tank can be seen behind them. Spring 1941.

▼ A Ustaša motorcyclist riding a single-seater Alce Guzzi. This man was a member of the security detail tasked with escorting Slavko Kvaternik, minister of the Armed Forces of the Independent State of Croatia. Bjelovar (Croatia), 1 November 1941 (HPM).

▲ A Ustaša tanker from the Black Legion poses in front of his small CV35, during a lull in a mopping-up action conducted in the Donji Vakuf region in 1942 (MNRH).

▼ A Ustaša armored unit fought in Herzegovina in the summer of 1944. The two officers posing in front of the Panzer I are Colonel Franjo Šimić of Domobranci and Captain Raphale Boban of Ustaša (HPM).

▲ Tankers of an unidentified Ustaša Brigade pictured in front of a French built Renault R-35: it is likely a tank which previously served with the dissolved Yugoslavian Royal Army (HPM).

▼ German and Croatian motorized elements in action during the spring-summer 1942 offensive. Both L3/35 light tanks in the foreground, supplied by Italy, belonging to a Ustaša Brigade, are trying to rescue a German Hotchkiss H35 tank immobilized in the mud.

▲ An unknown model of Yugoslavian armored vehicle captured by the Wehrmacht during the offensive on the Kozara mountains in August 1942: it could be one of the armored cars identified as "SPA", of which nothing is known (B.A.).

▼ A truck protected by improvised armor plates serving with a Croatian Ustaša unit, presumably the Black Legion, in Herzegovina. This type of armored vehicle, called "Oklopni Samovoz", was armed with a Schwarzlose machine gun. The vehicle's turret sports the Ustaša symbol. The Croatian state's crest was painted on the hull sides.

▲ Rear view of a "Samovoz" truck, equipped with handcrafted armor, used by Croatian Ustaša in Herzegovina (Znaci).

▼ The symbol painted on the turret was repeated on the armored truck sides, above the Croatian state's crest (Authors' Archive).

▲ Another picture showing one of the improvised armored trucks employed by Ustaša forces (Authors' Archive).

▼ Another armored truck of the "Black" Legion, with a large number 1 painted on the turret, photographed in the Prozor area in March 1943. General Pekic and Colonel Boban can be seen in front of the vehicle (HPM).

▲ A "Samovoz" armored truck pictured after being captured by Tito's partisans in Kordun (HPM).

▲ Ustaša armored column, during the celebration of the second anniversary of Croatian independence. The first vehicle is a CV33 of Hungarian origin mounting the typical commander cupola planned for tanks destined to Hungary. Even the machine gun is Hungarian (Benvenuti).

▼ The unit's vehicles parading in the presence of the Poglavnik Ante Pavelić, standing on the stage (Benvenuti).

▲ Another image from the same ceremony: the tank was manufactured in Italy, as witnessed by its armament (Benvenuti).

▼ Armored unit composed of German and Ustaša troops. The tank in the foreground, a Hotchkiss H39, appears painted in sand yellow overall.

▲ A L6/40 tank, taken from the Italians immediately after the Armistice, appears on the front cover of a 1944 issue of "Ustaša" magazine, published by Ante Pavelić's militia ("Ustaša").

▲ A column of L3 tanks belonging to a Ustaša Brigade move in January 1944. This picture was taken during an anti-partisan operation conducted in the Zumberak area. Note that these vehicles are finished in an overall green camouflage and show the emblem of Pavelić's formation on the front hull (HPM).

▼ A Ustaša L6/40 ready to move, pictured before a mopping-up operation.

▲ Although not mentioned in any official documents, this photograph testifies the use of Italian AB41 armored cars by Croatian armed forces. This vehicle, probably serving with the Poglavnik Guards, was pictured in Varaždin in 1944.

▼ Another L6/40 of the Ustaša; a smaller L3 can be seen in the background.

▲ Improvised armored vehicle, probably used for Ustaša crews training.

▼ Bad quality picture from a contemporary newspaper showing a column of Croatian L6/40 tanks.

▲ A beautiful image of a Ustaša L3/35 in Varazdin on 25 January 1944. The tank, without any markings, looks quite worn.

▼ The Armored Platoon of the 3rd Croatian Domobranci Military District, with a strength of 7 TK-3 tankettes, lined up to be reviewed. Sarajevo, 27 May, 1944.

▲ Ustaša elements during a mopping-up operation. The tanks shown here are Italian built L3s; the uniforms worn by tankers and militiamen are Italian made clothing.

▼ A gunner from the Croatian National Guard training in Germany. Note the French-made helmet, bearing the Croatian state's crest, hanging from his belt (Nationaal Archief).

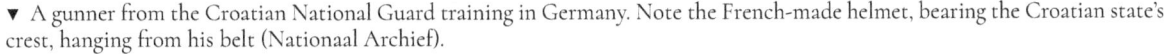

▲ Group photograph of Ustaša and Domobranci tankers posing aboard a Renault R-35.

▼ A Ustaša column composed of L6/40 tanks and Italian trucks move in the main street of a Croatian village.

▲ An Ustaša tank crew portrayed next to an L3. Winter 1944-45.

▲ In some cases the Germans installed the Panzer 38 (t) turret on the Italian M15/42 hull. One of this modified tanks, used by the Ustaša Obrana, is seen here moving in the snow. The vehicle, finished in a three-tone camouflage, has the Ustaša emblem and the plate UO 139. Winter 1944-1945.

▼ A L6/40 of Ustaša Obrana pictured in the last period of the war. The plate assigned to the tank is UO 128. The Ustaša emblem is painted on the hull front.

▲ A Croatian armored train captured by Tito's partisans, photographed in Kakanj on March 30, 1945.

▼ A line drawing published in the magazine of Pavelić's militia, representing a Croatian L6/40 tank: the vehicle's profile allows to identify the various positions of the Croatian state's crest on the vehicle, in accordance with guidelines applicable in the second half of the conflict ("Ustaša").

▲ Another drawing from "Ustaša" magazine, representing a L6 of a Pavelić's Brigade followed by a FIAT 665 NM Protetto Italian built truck used by Croatian militiamen. Such scenes are testified in some contemporary films ("Ustaša").

▼ Rare tank driver metal badge handed out to Ustaša personnel authorized to drive tanks. The badge encompassed all the traditional symbols universally linked to armored units, the tank and the wings, as well as the emblem of Pavelić's militia, with the "U" painted in deep blue.

▲ Tankers of the Black Legion immortalized with their L3 chariot. Region of Donji Vakuf (Bosnia), 1942 (HPM).

▲ The coat of arms of the Independent State of Croatia Armed Forces. The insignia put together the checkerboard shield, historical symbol of Croatia made up of 25 white and red squares, with the emblem of the Ustaša militia, the first armed force of the new Croatian state. This same coat of arms was painted on armored vehicles serving with Ustaša and Domobranci units.

▲ Ustaša metal badges, also commonly worn by militia tankers: an identical badge was worn on the cap.

▲ Close-up of an armored car turret used by the Ustaša. The symbol of the Croatian Ustaša can be seen in detail (authors' archive).

▼ Another beautiful image of the armored car in force at the Ustaša (HPM).

▲ Croatian National Guard Panzer I light wagon.

▼ L3 of Ustaša Obrana marked U. O. 123 (HDA).

▲ L6 of Ustaša Obrana (HDA).

▼ A L3 wagon and two Guzzi Trialce trucks used by the Ustaša troops.

▲ L3 in force at the Wagons Company of the 5th Ustaša Brigade.

▼ An L3 photographed in Zagreb during the oath ceremony of Ustaša students. On the left is Poglavnik Ante Pavelic (HPM).

▲ Establishment Ceremony of the Independent State of Croatia.

▼ The Croatian National Guard received some vehicles from the German Armed Forces to reinforce its logistic structure.

▲ Croatian National Guard soldier in front of St. Mark's Church in Zagreb: interesting is the use of the German helmet with the Croatian shield.

▲ Croatian National Guard tank Hotchiss H39, photographed in the spring of 1943.

▼ Ustaša armored truck photographed near Sarajevo in early 1943 (HDM).

▲ Close-up of an Ustaša soldier.

▲ An improvised convoy train set up to take these soldiers of the Croatian National Guard into a partisan-infested area.

▼ P.S.T. and Black Legion tanks photographed during Operation Weiss (HDM).

▲ On board of this Italian L2 wagon we find a war correspondent, who follows the military operation: he wears the inevitable camera (HDM) around his neck.

CROATIAN ARMORED UNITS DEPENDENT ON THE GERMAN ARMED FORCES

The German-Croatian Legion consisted of the 369. (Kroatische) Infanterie-Division, the 373. (Kroatische) Infanterie-Division and the 392. (Kroatische) Infanterie-Division. These formations were in all respects units of the Wehrmacht, made up of a large number of Croatian and Croatian Volksdeutschen soldiers, equipped with German uniforms and weapons, commanded by German officers. The Independent State of Croatia had absolutely no authority or control over them. Each of the three divisions had its own Panzerjäger-Abteilung, whose nominal strength was 6 Italian L40 self-propelled guns. The contingent situation, in fact, meant that each Panzerjäger-Abteilung was equipped with a limited number of assorted armor, mainly Italian built vehicles.
The Germans also nicknamed these formations "Schachbrett" ("Chessboard"), with reference to the typical red and white chequered shield of Croatia, which the volunteers of the Divisions wore on the right shoulder of the uniform.

369. (Kroatische) Infanterie-Division (369. (Hrvatska) Pješacka Divizija)

It consisted of around 3,500 German officers, non-commissioned officers and specialized personnel and 8,500 volunteer soldiers, all recruited by the Independent State of Croatia. Established on September 21, 1942 in Stockerau, the unit began training in Döllersheim in Austria.
Although originally intended for the Russian front, the 369th Division was transferred to Yugoslavia, where it took part in operation "Weiss", a major offensive launched against Tito's communist partisans. The unit was definitively used in the anti-partisan struggle conducted in the Croatian and Bosnian territories. It was also known as the "Devil's Division" (German: "Teufels Division" - Croatian: "Vražja Divizija"), because it distinguished itself for aggression and brutal behavior during the harsh campaign against Yugoslavian partisans.
The Panzerjäger-Abteilung 369 had 10 L3 tanks, 2 L6/40 tanks, 5 47/32 L40 self-propelled guns, 2 AB41 armored cars and, as demonstrated by photographs, at least 3 French tanks. In April 1945, after having suffered heavy losses, the Division was reduced to a Kampfgruppe armed with only 4 L40 self-propelled guns.

373. (Kroatische) Infanterie-Division (373. (Hrvatska) Pješacka Divizija)

It was established on June 6, 1943 with Croatian volunteers from a Croatian National Guard Brigade and with German officers, non-commissioned officers and specialists. The Division was trained at the Truppenübungsplatz Döllersheim[19]. Instead of being sent to the eastern front as initially planned, the unit was transferred to Yugoslavia, where it was deployed in the western areas of the country. Employed in the fight against the partisans in Yugoslavia until the end of the conflict, this formation was involved in the failed attempt to kill (or capture)

---
19 Military Training Area of Döllersheim.

Josip Broz (Tito), in May 1944. Initially made up of two Infantry Regiments, in the autumn of 1944 the Division absorbed the 2nd Jäger Brigade of the Croatian National Guard, which became the third Regiment of the unit.

Fallen out of the ranks due to desertions, the Division began to retreat north, towards the Reich, in the last days of April 1945, to finally surrender to the partisans between Brežice and Raka, in present-day Slovenia, on May 10, 1945.

The Panzerjäger-Abteilung of the 373. Croatian "Tiger" Division (German: "Tiger Division" - Croatian: "Tigar Divizija") initially had a L3 tank, a L6 tank and 9 L40 self-propelled guns; at the end of 1944 it had 2 AS37 Protetto armoured personnel carriers, 2 Italian armored cars, 12 L3s, 6 L6s and 10 L40 self-propelled guns.

392. (Kroatische) Infanterie-Division *(392. (Hrvatska) Pješacka Divizija)*

This unit was established on August 17, 1943 at the Truppenübungsplatz Döllersheim with voluntary Croatian soldiers, partly from the Croatian National Guard, and German cadres. It was initially intended for the eastern front, but was actually engaged in Croatian territory in anti-partisan operations until the end of the war. The Division freed the island of Korčula from partisans and defended the northern Adriatic coast and Lika, a traditional Croatian region. Desertion plagued this formation: many Croatian soldiers, disillusioned with the course of the war and incited by Tito agents, promising amnesty for deserters, began to mutiny in September 1944. In the last days of the war the Division received orders to retreat and to make its way to southern Austria, but surrendered in the Rijeka area.

Also known as the "Blue" Division (German: "Blaue Divison" - Croatian "Plava Divizija"), the unit had 2 L3s, 3 L6s and 7 self-propelled L40 guns in the 2nd Squadron of the Aufklärungs-Abteilung 392, operating on the Dalmatian coast.

▲ The sleeve patch, common to Croatian volunteers enrolled in the German Armed Forces, which earned the Croatian units the nickname "Schachbrett" ("Chess-board").

▲ Tanks from the Panzerjäger-Abteilung 369 of the 369th "Devil's Division" moving in the village of Gotovuša, Kosovo, in May-June 1943.

▼ Croatian P.T.S. tank crews climb aboard a German Pzkpfw IV Ausf G medium tank. Germany, 1944 (B.A.).

▲ Croatian tankers trained in Germany. These men wore uniforms with Ustaša insignia (B.A.).

▼ A photograph showing a Krupp Protze truck with a Pak 38 50 mm anti-tank gun in tow from the 369th Croatian Division fallen into the hands of Yugoslavian partisans. Vicinity of Nevesinje (Bosnia and Herzegovina), February 1945 (Znaci).

▲ The regimental flag is awarded to the 369th Regiment in the presence of Minister Ivica Frković. Ante Pavelić's monogram stands out in the middle of the flag. Mostar, 18 April, 1944.

▼ Croatian tank crew training aboard a PzKpfw IV Ausf G. The tank in the background is a Pzkpfw III Ausf N.

▲ Close-up of a Croatian tank commander aboard a PzKpfw IV Ausf G. This photograph makes you to appreciate some important details of the uniform.

▲ The crew members of a Pzkpfw IV, all Croatian tankers, listen to the recommendations of a German instructor.

SLOVENIAN ARMORED FIGHTING VEHICLES

In 1941, Slovenia was divided between Germany, Italy (which established the so-called Ljubljana Province) and Hungary. As in the rest of Yugoslavia, even in Slovenia an active movement of resistance to Nazifascism, established under the denomination of AVNOJ (Antifašistični svet narodne osvoboditve Jugoslavije), has been active since 1943. In September of the same year, following the Italian surrender, all Slovenian territory was occupied by German troops, thus passing under the direct control of the Gauleiter of Carinthia, F. Rainer. In the same month, a voluntary collaborationist militia, the Slovenian Territorial Guard (Slovensko Domobranstvo), was created to support the German Armed Forces in the struggle against the Yugoslavian People's Liberation Army. Leon Rupnik, former general of the Yugoslavian Army, was the Commander of the Domobranci militia, which gradually assumed increasing operational autonomy and grew to a strenght of 13,000 men; it was equipped by the Germans with weapons seized from the Italians after the Armistice of 1943 and was trained by the German SS. Between April and May 1945, Slovenia was occupied by Resistance units of the Slovenian IX Corpus and like many Croatian soldiers, most of the Domobranci, prisoners of the British Eighth Army near Klagenfurt, were delivered to the EPLJ (Yugoslavian People's Liberation Army) thus facing mass summary executions.

If the Croatian units managed to set up fairly organic armored units, the armored component of the Slovenian armed forces was much reduced. At the end of the summer of 1944 the Domobranci obtained from the Germans an unspecified number of 47/32 L40 self-propelled guns, some of which were of late production, distinguishable by a modified and enlarged superstructure and armed with a Breda 38 machine gun, protected by a shield, mounted at the front. The vehicles were used by detachments located in the vicinity of Lubiana and, according to a partisan document dating from the end of 1944, the Domobranci could count on 6 "tanks", probably all L40 self-propelled guns, placed under the command of Ordnungspolizei Pol. Pz. Kp . 14.

The Domobranci forces also used various improvised armored trucks of Italian origin and supplied crews for some armored trains operating in Slovenian territory.

Colors of Slovenian armored fighting vehicles

Slovenian L40 self-propelled guns were painted in sand yellow with large green and, probably, brown (a non-standard Italian camouflage, probably painted over the sand yellow color applied by the Germans) spots; like Croatian tankmen, even Slovenian crews made use of Dutch tanker suits, items coming from the spoil taken by the Wehrmacht during the invasion of Netherlands in 1940.

▲ Beautiful image of one 47/32 L40 Italian self propelled guns of the Slovenian Domobranci, appeared on the cover of No. 5 Issue of "Slovensko Domobrantsvo", the unit magazine. (Slovensko Domobrantsvo).

▲ Other pictures of the same self-propelled gun, printed in the magazine. This is a late production L40, characterized by a modified casemate, supplied by the German Armed Forces along with other vehicles in the second half of 1944 (Slovensko Domobrantsvo).

▲ An OM Taurus truck with improvised armor, fully loaded with militiamen, moves forward during the same action depicted in the previous photos. The vehicle's plate, "Slov.D. 56", apparently seems hand-painted (Slovensko Domobrantsvo).

▲ A Domobranci SPA CL39 Italian built light truck photographed in Ljubljana; the vehicle, still sporting its original grey-green color, had the plate "SD 26" (Slovensko Domobrantsvo).

▼ The oath ceremony of the Domobranci at Bežigrad stadium, Ljubljana, on 20 April 1944. Domobranci units and police departments swore allegiance to the Slovenian nation in the presence of Rupnik (pictured in civilian clothes), head of the Province government, and SS general Erwin Rösener.

▲ Domobranci self-propelled guns pictured during the oath ceremony at the Bežigrad stadium in Ljubljana The vehicle in the background seems to have a standard casemate type, not enlarged. It is known that camouflage patches were of two different colors, probably brown and green.

▲ Domobranci and policemen lined up at the Bežigrad stadium in Ljubljana. The Slovenian national flag which had been abolished during the Italian occupation was hoisted for the first time. The coat of arms of the Carniola region was also displayed on this occasion.

▼ Artillerymen of the Domobranci 3rd Battery stationed in Velike Lašče, Slovenia (Slovensko Domobrantsvo).

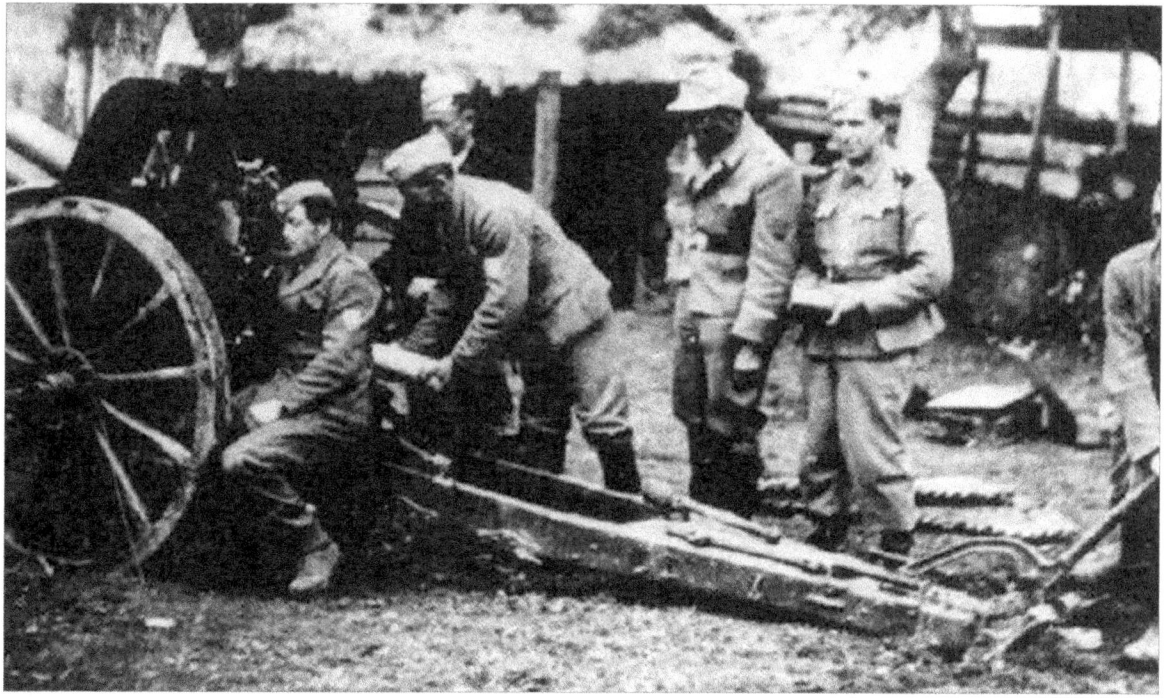

▲ Domobranci sleeve patch.

Bibliography

- Babac Dušan, "Elitni vidovi jugoslovenske vojske u Aprilskom ratu", Evoluta, Belgrado, 2008.
- Barlozzetti Ugo, Pirella Alberto, "Mezzi dell'Esercito italiano 1935 – 1945", Editoriale Olimpia, Firenze, 1986.
- Benvenuti Bruno, Colonna Ugo, "Fronte Terra", volumi 1, 2/I, 2/II e 2/III, Edizioni Bizzarri, Roma, 1974.
- Cappellano Filippo, Pignato Nicola, "Gli autoveicoli da combattimento dell'Esercito Italiano", volumi I e II, S.M.E. – Ufficio Storico, Roma, 2002.
- Ceva Lucio, Curami Andrea, "La meccanizzazione dell'Esercito fino al 1943", S.M.E – Ufficio Storico, Roma, 1989.
- Corbatti Sergio, Nava Marco, "Come il diamante", Laran Editions, Bruxelles, 2008.
- Di Colloredo Mels Pierluigi Romeo, "Controguerriglia – La 2° Armata italiana e l'occupazione dei Balcani 1941 – 1943", Luca Cristini Editore, 2019, Bergamo.
- Di Giusto Stefano, "I reparti Panzer nell'Operationszone Adriatisches Kustenland", Edizioni della Laguna, Mariano del Friuli (GO), 2002.
- Guglielmi Daniele, "Italian Armour in German Service 1943 – 1945", Mattioli 1885, Parma, 2005.
- L. da Zeng, "Croatian Armor: a discussion", 2012.
- Mollo Andrew, "Le Forze Armate della Seconda Guerra Mondiale – uniformi, distintivi e organizzazione", Istituto Geografico De Agostini, Novara, 1982.
- Munoz Antonio J., "Slovenian Axis Forces in World War II 1941 - 1945", Axis Europa Books, Bayside (USA).
- Pignato Nicola, "Un secolo di autoblinde in Italia", Mattioli 1885, Parma, 2008.
- Potocnick Gregor, "Slovensko Domobranstvo", Lubiana, 2013.
- Predoević Dinko, "Oklopna vozila i oklopne postrojbe u drugom svjetskom ratu u Hrvatskoj - I.dio", Adamic – Digital Point Tiskara, Rijeka (HR), 2002.
- Predoević Dinko, "Oklopna vozila i oklopne postrojbe u drugom svjetskom ratu u Hrvatskoj - II.dio", Adamic – Digital Point Tiskara, Rijeka (HR), 2008.
- Predoević Dinko, Dimitrijević Bojan, "Oklopne postrojbe Sila Osovine na jugoistoku Europe u Drugome svjetskom ratu", Despot Infinitus d.o.o., Zagabria (HR), 2015.
- Tallillo Antonio, Tallillo Andrea, Guglielmi Daniele "Carro L3 – Carri veloci, carri leggeri, derivati", G.M.T., Trento, 2004.
- Tallillo Antonio, Tallillo Andrea, Guglielmi Daniele, "Carro L6 – Carri leggeri, semoventi e derivati", G.M.T., Trento, 2007.

• Thomas Nigel, Mikulan Krunoslav, "Axis Forces in Yugoslavia 1941 – 45", collana "Men at Arms" n° 282, Osprey Publishing, Oxford (UK), 2001.
• Zaloga Steve, "Tanks of Hitler's Eastern Allies 1941 – 1945", New Vanguard n° 199, Osprey Publishing, Oxford (UK), 2013.
• Zaloga Steve "The Eastern Front, Armour Camouflage & Markings", Arms and Armour Press, 1983.
• Yann Mahè, "Croatie 1941 -1945" in "Batailles et Blindes" n° 42 – aprile/maggio 2011, Caraktére, Aix-enProvence (F).

TITOLI GIÀ PUBBLICATI
TITLES ALREADY PUBLISHING

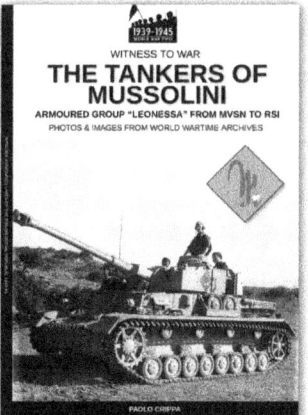
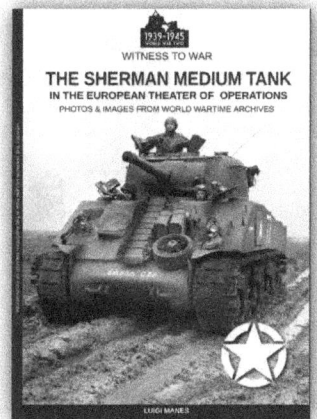

www.ingramcontent.com/pod-product-compliance
Lightning Source LLC
LaVergne TN
LVHW081545070526
838199LV00057B/3785